JN411151

Rock Is Thunder

Rock Is Thunder

A collection of new poems by Lee Jae hoon
Translated by Susan K

K
POET

아시아

Contents

ROCK IS THUNDER

The Obsolete

It's a time for the senses,
only the click-clacking footsteps loud and clear.
Roots spread on and on to the sides.
They can't steal, but they try.
It's a time for debauchery.

Would you do it if you turned into a pig?
The traces have been neglected.
Rocks have aged ears.
Chatters come from schools, markets, bars.
Words of mockery.
What clans made me this way?
I'm still an obsolete person

brimming with uncertainties.
I'm drunk on darkness, and just in time
it starts to rain.
I can't kill myself.

I'm obsolete,
can't talk about what I see or hear.
Just an obsolete person.

Rocks Made of Tears

The sun makes deserts,
clouds make rain,
tears make men.

Oh, writer of poems,
priest of tears.

Unable to take revenge
or change shapes,
rocks leave themselves to fate.

They only know the labor of rolling,
sharpening their bodies for a lifetime.

Rocks are made responsible for all earthly sins.
They throw, kick, bury, break,

given the penalty not to rot.
Their bodies remain silent,

brave enough to smash against
the air, sea, and ground.

It's a divine punishment, the body wandering
the universe
well before men's time, Earth's time.

From the Street, the Most Beautiful Street

Did you fool my eyes? I'm sunk in the deep sea. Scared of getting pricked, I can't go near. I walk into a different time. A bruise knows no harmony, only has bad memories. Does good arrest exist? I get on the car, chase the farthest eon. I meet trees and birds but brush past them. When I go past Daejeon, past Nonsan to Iksan, there are no birds, only the sky. Was anything good in the past? The sky darkens. I go past Jeongeup, Damyang, Gochang to Gwangju. Dusk comes. Evening glow fills the street. Namdo's not far now. I learn the streets from the street. You can't stand familiar things. You put up an umbrella, cover your eyes. You're not in the eon. You're across the water. From the street, the most beautiful street. Are you listening? Did you prepare a way to reach virtue? Are you a rock now?

A History of Rock's Disasters

Where were you born? The past is the past, a palace's memories and a beggar's memories alike.

You were all in your mother's arms before being on the ground. You didn't stop laughing even among the pack of wolves. You're not vain. You're a good person.

Do you know the way to the stable? You were in a vault, born in the streets, scarred by whips. You heard the bells before anyone else.

You've been in all fears—mighty land, endless sea. There are too many giants in this world.

Language is being corrupted. Revolution is the only truth. Do you use kind language? Be honest. All laments have a reason.

Envy, complaint, frustration, lust. Don't hide the language of suffering. If you want to comfort and celebrate, choose the best option. Great words mean sharing a dream.

From this mountain to that, in joyous footsteps, you roll your body in difficult, tricky words. You might run into silence if you keep going as a rock.

Rock Is Thunder

It flows from up high.
The sound pours out from our plea,
covers people
and wishes
and anger
and hard sins.
It's the sound of pebbles rolling.
Tears fill my head.
People shout in dialects
under the Samgaksan tree at dawn.
People fix their illness
slapping their bare flesh.
Sound gets ahead of time.
When it calls out, Mom,

it becomes the saddest beast.
When a rock struck the sky
long, long ago
lightning flashed and thunder rumbled.
A sound replied from above.
Having no place to cry,
I entered the rock.
My whole body whirs these days.

A Rock's Ordeal

Tied to a boat, I go against the rough waves. Time doesn't obey light. No order can restrain me. I don't want to remain bound, don't want to make a deal with nasty, obscene groups, those who brag about their errors. I sit resting my chin in my hand, think of your name.

Some people eat monkeys. I'd rather be a dull, hard being, a static being that doesn't cease to exist even when beaten, cracked, burst. I don't want to believe in the saying that a lack can be of help. Disturbing scars are left on the whipped body. I want my body to have no scars.

I want to gather the souls of those who died holding a golden cane. I tried to hold you in my arms, but you swept my body like smoke and left. Now all that remains of you is a shadow. Memories fill my eyes only when sunlight sprouts. How is the only way to live leaving humans? There's a body thrown down among many rocks, a body with no name, no matter how many times it rolls.

Bolt

What jewelry will come from the hundred billion galaxies? What's left of capitalism is fear, countless small people who struggle. Social media brims with those who show off gifts. We have the pleasure of seeing flowers if there's congestion on the road and find a road if there isn't one. I got to see the ceiling wallpaper when the roof leaked. I eat a late dinner, just tofu stew. There's nothing but the war on the news. It's raining. The flowerpot on the windowsill rattles. Feeling slightly empty, I fiddle with my smart phone.

A kiss isn't just a feeling. It's about bones and the moon rattling. It's a stormy evening, long after I'd left my hometown. With no place to return I've become a prisoner of the world, but I've got a folktale for you. I also have an eye for spotting deer, know the taste of stream water and a freshly-caught animal's blood.

Let them laugh. Those with a damaged soul read poetry. They wail, calling their friends and anxiety, boast in a loud voice. It's the day we see a shooting star, the day I return to another life, the day many stars blink and disappear.

Only the Unchanging Things Save Me

Worry comes over me.
I can't breathe. Blood doesn't circulate.
I keep the trash, unable to throw it away.
I charge my phone at night to remember the shame.

Half broken, half returned, I became poor.
People are only interested in what changes.

I find a forest,
put my lips on the water
and air that won't vanish.

Houses, cars, jobs, people all change.

Only the dusk and dawn don't.

Only poor things don't change.
The things I'll keep till I die save me.

I stare at the pebbles piled up in the flowerpot.
Impure lips turn clear.

Blue

My skin keeps drying. Sighs don't turn into songs but to germs, invade the skin. Drinking melts bones. I become a customary animal, sleep in the morning, work at night. It's because of those who suspect and aggravate. It's no use writing a letter, speaking with my eyes. The world's measuring me. My tongue's been cut out. I can't sing, the rhythm's been taken away. With my tongue gone, I can't call or lick you. I'm dizzy. Recollecting the past, I drink nostalgia.

Were you oppressed? I just wish the rice would cook. The exclusion must've been a special one. I'm living my unrecorded forties, a rock that gets tested each time. Cold air pierces my thighs. Is this world made of symbols? I wish I were someone's son or brother, someone's pupil, teacher, or lover. It's time for thorough apostasy. Mockery blows like strong wind. Have you been away for three years? Did you borrow love, didn't pay it back? Did you proffer the night?

Belonging to Stone

I get kicked by a jagged rock,
one that stood upright then got chipped.
Spear, blade, wind
must've sliced its body in half
when darkness was all around.
Only the eyes of those who dumped me in the street
flashed at night.
Sometimes a rock supports a being from under the feet.
When a rock supports my house,
my father's promise,
there's a trace of blood on it.
It may break but won't die.

Without a perishable body
it gets kicked, stepped on, stretched.
It watches every moment
the extinct and the birthplace become one.
It secretly inhabits your soul
that stays and leaves without a trace
when the world spins dizzily in the dark.
The stone of incarnation
makes a human face, the body of Jesus and Maria.
The stone on the road lives an eternal life
as someone made of stone,
a stone of thick truths.

Green Universe

I longed for a firm, large body.
The world only wanted big, strong things.
Heroes were those who stayed in their unluckiest state.
My body shone.
I took misfortunes and peculiarities as destiny,
which shone brighter because of the occasional joy.
I loved the sun that heated my body.
Human time is nothing.
Humans only eat, sleep, weep till the end,
weaklings who filthily lust for a tombstone.
I have crossed a light year, have a body of letters,

all the world's pain engraved on it.
The truly strong are the ones who watch in silence.
I'll hold a feast,
put down some roots, grow leaves and fruits.
You might be blinded by the bright green light my body emits.
You can't eat me even if you beg.
Instead I'll enter a human house, watch all the time.
I'll watch with a vivid life
what's called cutting-edge, civilization, art,
all the souls you left dying.

History

Rock is clear.
Engraving letters on it is a disgrace.
It's an object before humans,
a time of unknown origin.
People bow to the rock
where angel and devil dwell.
Rocks often fell from the sky.
Even outer world's time mixed with this one
in the rock of infinity.
I made arrowheads, axes with the rock,
killed animals, took their bodies,
killed the species, took other bodies,
buried mother's bones
which became a rock, rose from the ground.

Oblivious at first, it becomes obvious with
time.
All beings are born from dirt.
I throw a rock, hear a cry.
I throw a rock, my whole body's
nestled underground like a baby.
Those who break free from a rock,
those who miss their house of rock
all become a star
when a rock is thrown into the sky.

Erosion

Sunlight pushes its way in through the window. Its destiny is to shine only in the gap, a body that lives by a day's joy. Plants take the body and grow. A rock is under a flower tree that opens its mouth towards the sun. A body that can't even crawl or fly. The rock breathes ever so slowly, moves stealthily, unnoticed. Humans turn ash gray. They step on the rock, look at the sky. The rock hangs its head lowest under the shabby brick wall, lower than a dog's food bowl. There's no end to the hard life. To the rock that's slower than clouds, even the woods' lesson is useless, the dusk's comfort an eyesore. A rock's destiny doesn't lie in seasons or the wind that tells where the home is. Even the height of the tree that shares the blazing sun with the shade doesn't talk to the rock that faces the ground. The rock's body doesn't resent anyone. Its back can only be seen after jumping over human's time. When I wake up with no contradiction or anguish, the body's flown a lifetime.

A Pebble's Prayer

I had many hard things in me.
I climb a hill, watch the city.
Robbery, rape, suicide happen daily.
I've tried so hard to hide myself,
carefully crossed the summer with excuses and repentance.
Traps are everywhere.
It's easy to throw a stone, harder to hold one.
It's too hot or cold, too heavy or hard.
With a finger I write on the dirt.
Everyone wants to be cleared of their sins.
No one apologizes.

Can only absolute joy soften the heart?
A concealed sin makes a greater one.
A fish has no blocked paths.
There's no way to stop the misfortune that appears from nowhere.
Only pebbles fill my pockets,
pebbles I can't sell or give away.
With my pockets full of pebbles,
mouth full of hurtful words

I flop down holding a pebble in my arms,
look in the eyes of passersby.

Mirror

Forty years are crammed into a face-sized rock. Your drawings, your books, your windows, the family photo you stared at each day, the couch you slept on. Your alley, cold coffee.

Your face, colored oddly, remains expressionless. I always climbed the stairs and dreamt of falling at night. I liked the sound of breathing I heard as I climbed on. The sound of the river coming from afar, the cry that rolled up like a scroll.

A butterfly soars from the rock, flutters its wings before me. Dust falls from the wings into the snow.

The Ruins Lab

It's sharp. From here to there, from there to infinity, from one side to another it comes and goes as you and I. Our faces reflect on each other. You and your there. To there and over there it penetrates, inserts. From there to here, from this world to the next, from one time to another, it bends, splinters, as light, wind, air and water, from the past to the future, from the future to the present. I return. You float. Someone from the present, another from the future, your mirror, dear your mirror, fiction and fact, illusion and truth, void and mire, bluff and mire mix and mingle. Tests and announcements are tightened, coaxed onto your desk and chair. What is composition? What is creation? What is poetry, a rock? I want to eat your universe. I want to insert your face. I aim the bow, shoot time. Mirror, jewelry, white stone are stuck in the display window. Dream reflects as a rainbow, without boundary, white, yellow, clear. It remains a hard substance.

Seashore Stone

Stone is time's meal,
its timeworn skin cozy as flesh.

The story of becoming a pebble, the back of the silent man at the bar, the eyes of someone who wandered for long, the birthday morning coffee on an empty stomach, the red eyes of the late-night taxi driver, the sobering tweets of early birds, the hours recorded into the notebook, the chronology that hardens slowly…

When lingering feelings visit from time to time

all things build a house from their skin.
It's a sound of memories rolling its body.

I remember your eyes.
I remember your white teeth,

the rowdy metaphor

that's rolled and rolled
until disillusionment became nostalgia.

Cave Paintings

I put my ear on the wall, hear water running in the distance. I close my eyes, hear your voice. I've always longed for the distant—sounds of water, sounds of door. Listening to wet sounds my body becomes a sound. Exploration begins unexpectedly. In the stone wall are gaps here and there. In the gaps, darkness here and there. My body's sucked into the thin darkness. It doesn't become a rock or history but a shapeless, formless flabby love juice of lust that burns in a rock. A fish swims in it, flapping its fins. The rock shakes. I'm out of breath, singing in the rock, in the water in the rock. Water enters the holes in my body. My skin turns bumpy and hard. My whole body turns to water. The moment I turn to stone underwater, I dream of water turning to stone. Water splashes from far in the body that's turned to stone.

Ashes' Joy

I walk the hallway with eyes closed. Unable to run, I feel my way from one room to another. I find clothes. History needs a stage. I fall if I stand like a bicycle. I want to be alone, a miracle to happen. Music plays from the smart phone. Sharp, annoying words and fake smiles float down the street. Perhaps what I want are all useless, I shouldn't hear anything. Love spreads like fire or wind, rises in the sky. It's like having my clothes torn, letting go of the irrevocable violent memory, chained to a scar and always crying, holding the hand of a child that's crying in split time. Hard things scatter as ashes, fly into the clouds.

The Story of Misreading

My beginning was always coincidental. There was light, water, sky, one who breathed underwater. No one's ever taught me the mystique of water, the time of rocks. I kick lazily with the memory of a faraway land.

I've wronged you. My heart as collateral, I viewed all customs of the world as worthless. I crossed my fingers and dreamt, all the while sending you razor-sharp words. So I thought I could forget you now.

Maybe defensive words were merely a dream. I thought of a room that's peaceful even in the storm. When water droplets entered, I forgot all about the marriage dream, gasping, flailing.

I watched your back from afar, wanted to replace your wrinkled collar and stained sleeve. Deep dark night, I should've just stared at the stars. My little crumbling dolor is like a gently floating paper boat.

The night is thick with misreading. I can't see me. I hope it was forgiveness you read. I've lived by the razor-sharp words you'd said to me, became a hard body that's being shaved for millions of years. The night reminds me of you who has the word "forgiveness."

POET'S NOTE

Taking Care of a Rock

The subject of a poem comes suddenly like destiny. The first subjects I encountered with emphasis were snow and stars—snow pallets and faraway planets, to be exact. Subjects are always mundane. How used up are the subjects of snow and stars?

I've wandered in search for various subjects, floating in the void of space, strolling through the medieval ruins. I've glimpsed at the edge of a myth, roamed the streets of a city. I got lost not only in subjects but in spaces like the Yellow River and Inca civilization, Norse mythology, trees, dirt, and cities.

Then I met rocks, came back to the mundane.

Rock is such a mundane subject. I didn't dare write poems about them. I didn't dare, but I still wrote them. I couldn't help it, couldn't stop poems from gushing out. Like destiny I kept writing poems about rocks. I wanted to talk about origins and essences. It's impossible to tell a rock's time. It has no owner. It's in disdain, in worship. It abandons, collects, covers, hides. It exists all around the world. I wrote poems in hopes of asking a rock. Asking questions made me feel sorry for it, made me feel for it.

A rock is a great substance. The deeper I encountered it, the further it veered away from me. And the greater the distance, the fonder my heart grew. Jacob from the Bible had a dream in which he used a stone as a pillow. His sins and sorrow turned into a blessing through the dream. I hope the rock can be a blessing, not sorrow. I hope it can be a comfort, not purgation or repentance. Poems I wrote in order to encounter such rocks gathered little by little. This will also be a period in my life. If something helps me endure it, that'll be my destiny.

POET'S ESSAY

About Superfluity

*

Once I translate the intuition I happen to realize into language, it becomes insignificant, often ends up as plain fragments of thoughts. The same goes when I face splendid scenery. It's too shabby when it turns to language. Oftentimes it's better to imagine a conversation in a dream or ultimate scenery I haven't seen in real life. Reality or truth isn't such a simple matter. Only after it survives the most painful, agonizing time from up close can it contain a corner of its soul.

*

I used to think that the sky was made of stone, for sometimes rocks fell from it. I thought of meteors in that way. A rock is an old substance that humans could commonly see from up close. Many myths claim that the first human was born from a rock. Its primeval temporality still remains in actuality. Compared to stone, human time is extremely short. Perhaps that's why humans bow to stone, make God statues with it. That's the reason a stone's imagination lingers around my poems for a while.

*

I don't have the talent to work out a poem. Nor do I have a profound philosophy or the wisdom to accept. I'm only filled with the desire to write poetry, sense of identity as a writer of poetry, will to not become a profiteer in disguise as a poet. I also ache to draw my own picture instead of furtively copying what others do. I embrace my heart that fills up with poetry. I push forward, relying solely on my poor heart, and write.

*

Poetry has the destiny to pursue the unfinished. Perfect poetry doesn't exist in this world. A poem's never enough, always has a point of criticism. This unfinished destiny becomes the force to write another poem.

*

I don't write poetry to persuade others or to get evaluated. Writing poetry is an act of pouring out my soul, my vain, shameless, suffering, sometimes proud soul, most ardently and urgently. I have no choice but to keep hearing words of persuasion or evaluation, however. I take in those words with loving care, brood over them, reconsider, because poetry's not a diary but an intentional movement towards another being, because my poems are not a profound scripture but a confession of a corrupted individual.

*

So far I've rapidly unfolded space and time. From the beginning of time to the present, from the earth to space. I've been told that I fly too much, but these journeys are necessary for me. I'll now sink underground or dig into a rock. I've come to realize that time might begin anew from those places.

*

Something always remains after I write a poem. It doesn't fill up no matter how much effort I put into it. Something remains, and that margin shames me. It's an odd feeling, a mixture of remorse and anticipation for a new poem. That power of superfluity makes me consider poetry, crave it desperately.

*

Eternal subjects of my literature are gods and myths. We don't fully trust any absolute being, yet we rely embarrassingly on them, praying, crying, complaining, devoting. The greediest, most honorable and disgraceful—sometimes reckless—sacrificial things originate from the relationship between god and human. Even atheists can't be free from god's existence when they're in trouble. Myths are stories about human nature. They openly depict the frustration outside the door to every good and evil, instinct and redemption. And through that frustration we dream of being born once more.

*

"Poetry is beautiful" implies that it's sad, doleful. Like this rainy spring night I'm drinking alone, reading Szymborska.

*

Hiding and showing, action and reaction, calm and commotion, stopping and moving, flowing and rising, dropping and soaring, angel and devil, home and far, nature and civilization, macho and feminist, progressive and conservative, future and past, Kim Suyeong and

Kim Chunsu. Tension in poetry occurs when these binary oppositions target and fight against each other. Poetry is dazzling when that tension is retained till the final moment. But sometimes there are rare sceneries like Park Yongrae's. It's the tension of mixture not battle that remains more beautifully in one's heart.

*

I think long and hard each time whether it would be better to imagine a target or imagine me who imagines. They may sound the same, but poets will know that they'll lead to completely different poems.

*

Poetry no longer tries to please its readers. Rather, it tries to please its poet companions and critics. It's a bitter experience, trying to please someone. It denotes a lack of certainty, like confirming that you're inferior. If you don't try to please others, you're viewed as self-righteous. Would it be possible to try to please in moderation? In other words, poetry doesn't try to please; it's just lonely. Could it be that it just wants to be understood?

*

Space is crucial in writing poetry. Sometimes I write lying on the floor or at a bus stop. Sometimes I write in my memo pad or in my notebook. These days I often use the memo app on my smart phone. When I'm unable to create a special space, I turn my space into a special one. I call my room the Kafka Study. It only turns into a study after eleven p.m. I sit at the desk like I'm Kafka. I make up my mind to scribble something at least, but I end up falling asleep, telling myself that even Kafka couldn't have stopped himself.

*

No one writes a poem knowing the final line. Even if they have it written in advance, the ending always changes. In some cases the rhythm of the sentences move in sync and weaves the poem against my will. In other cases one line calls the next, which then calls another one, and the poem completes itself. Or sometimes a muse comes, writes a poem for me. But she stopped coming ever since I turned forty. My Muse, I've waited too long for you. Please come by sometime.

*

Singing or praising nature is a very old tradition. The only classical work of poetry is nature. I'm just not there yet, but I too will become a classicist one day.

*

There's no better condition to write poetry than in indulgence. Infatuation ferments time, which then explodes as words. Language bursts out when I obsess over a thing or part ways with it. A poet must go through many breakups. To do that, we must be in love, either with a person, an animal, or nature. What kind of love am I in right now? Is it with a rock or the obscure morning fog?

*

Nowadays studying or playing is more prevalent among us than singing, complimenting, or praising. Everyone's engaged in philosophy or wordplay in poetry. Even if they want to sing or praise, there's no object. God doesn't listen to the prayers of the poor, and heroes have long been gone. Nature reeks, and humans are hideous. It's surprising that the world is brimming with love songs despite all that. I guess humans can't live without love.

*

I often feel the gap in dreams between one who writes poetry and one who reads it. The one writing wants to create words of self-reliance and enlightenment. The one reading is not interested in enlightenment but captivated by the sentimental rhetoric that speaks directly to the reader. But once a poet feels sentimentality from his language, he tries immediately to veer away from that moment.

*

It is awfully misleading to declare the exploration of ego autistic. Poetry is the word of shamans. Shamans who write poetry get frequently ill and are always in pain. Even poems that speak of social reality often go through an individual's convalescence. Our community can be viewed through a collection of each and every problematic ego. Serious exploration of ego is the most straightforward writing of poetry, since a poet's more like a problematic individual than a teacher that reforms the world.

*

Our poetry's excessively wallowed in sadness, as if happiness violates the ethics of poetry. But we still have many things to be sad about. Perhaps all of this sadness will be resolved if we grieve for hundreds of years. Poetry might vanish if it comes when there are more reasons to be happy than sad.

*

Poetry discovers many things. It discovers the holy in the ugliest place, the ugliest in the holiest place. Like seeing the universe through one speck of dust, it reminds us of the greatest thing through the smallest and transforms the greatest thing into the most insignificant nothing.

*

Poetry is a genre of the signified. What gets lost when the signified actively plays around in amusement is the purpose of amusement. A game without a clear purpose is extremely difficult. One must subtly read whether it's trying to tease, ridicule, criticize, or win. Of course there are games of which the purpose is to not have a purpose. There are many games without a reason in this world. Not all games are fun or emotional.

*

I've once heard while drinking that there's no change in poetry without a change in life. It means to change life to change poetry. But poets who have actually tried changing their life are against it, because there's a chance that life can make poetry shabby, destitute. Each must have a place in life where they can maintain self-respect as a poet. It's fine as long as one can find that familiar spot. I wouldn't complain if I could write poetry greeting the sunset every day in a spot that's not too high or low. Perhaps I'm still searching for that spot where I belong, the life spot where I can retain self-respect as a poet.

COMMENTARY

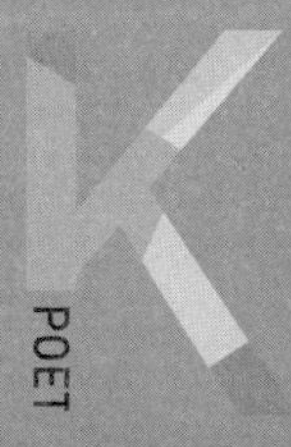

Once More Raising the Beings that Could but Turn to Stone

Oh Eun (Poet)

"Every block of stone has a statue inside it, and it is the task of the sculptor to discover it."

—Michelangelo Buonarroti

Words are everywhere. They spread, become rumors and arguments, and then settle as strong beliefs. Among clamors and murmurs they all raise their voices to prove their existence. *I'm here, listen to me, come stand by me.* There's no room for silence. Lee Jae hoon lends his ears to silent beings in his poetry collection *Rock is Thunder*. To be precise, he opens the mouth of the silent. It's to cut a sedimentary rock open, to open a Pandora's box, to give air to the beings that are thought not to exist. This gentle, refreshing work is like bursting open the unique stories inside a rock, once more raising the beings that could but turn to stone. It's returning the forgotten name to its owner.

The first poem in the collection is "The Obsolete." An obsolete person confesses that it's "a time for the senses," "a time for debauchery," "the traces have been neglected," that he's "brimming with uncertainties," and "can't kill [him]self." I have no choice but to remain silent among the "words of mockery," because the obsolete becomes closer to the past each and every day, because new people slowly fill the gap as if nothing had happened. Even in the merciless oblivion of the world, the senses of the obsolete sharpen more and more. The body of the obsolete is an "aged ear[]," a sensory organ. The obsolete and the rock share one body, one heart. The obsolete who "can't talk about what [he] see[s] or hear[s]" is always quiet, appears to be still. At least from the outside. Only from the outside.

As a sculptor discovers a statue inside a stone, the poet who is a "priest of tears" must hear the words contained in his ears again, must become voluntarily sharp as the obsolete. He must understand the stance of rocks that are "unable to take revenge or change shapes." He must look straight into the surface of rocks where "all earthly sins" are engraved and observe the inner side of rocks with the "penalty not to rot." Hence "the body wandering the universe" in the poem "Rocks Made of Tears" is placed again before us. Rocks have always been in their spot, but their status has changed in kindness. Kicked, thrown, sat on, rocks are finally able to tell their inside story, show their history of disasters. Rocks, which have become both general and independent beings, must prove their existential crisis with the entire body.

A rock is a hard mass of minerals that is formed by hardened dirt and other substances, but it can't necessarily be defined as solid. The poet realizes in "Rock Is Thunder" that "tears fill [his] head" even at the "sound of pebbles rolling" because a rock is a place to enter when he "[has] no place to cry." In order to know a rock, we must listen to the lament in "A History of Rock's Disasters" that pour out words of "envy, complaint, frustration, [and] lust" that had been busy hiding till then. A rock is both solid and liquid, a wave and a sound. Therefore, the expression "throwing rocks" that means "to criticize someone" could be interpreted as "to confess" if we consider the properties of a rock, for the rock has not been thrown by someone but been actively projected to prove itself. Therefore, watching a rock fly is like facing the story of a rock that couldn't but harden.

Meanwhile, a rock can also be a spokesperson of the weak in Lee's collection of poems. The obsolete couldn't talk because the timing's too early or too late, but rocks remain in a state of elimination or lagging from the systems of this world. They live as a "whipped body," "a body with no name (A Rock's Ordeal)" by those who are engrossed in "throw[ing], kick[ing], bury[ing], [and] break[ing] (Rocks Made of Tears)." They also become "a rock that gets tested each time" in front of "those who suspect and aggravate," as seen in "Blue." Rock is considered a punch bag, a common insignificant creature. It gets mocked even after a lifetime of silent labor. The word "obstacle," which means "a thing that blocks or hinders progress" represents a rock's position.

At the same time, a rock "may break but won't die." When it's said to exist as "a stone of thick truths," it doesn't simply refer to a pile of rocks. This thickness in "Belonging to Stone" means "someone made of stone," an anonymous person of solitude. Even when a rock is chipped, broken, or shattered due to external factors, the fact that it's a rock doesn't change. Nor does the story that's seeped through a rock. A rock multiplies in numbers as it breaks. It can shrink in size but never disappear from the earth. Humans aren't able to hear it, but grains of sand sparkle as they shout towards those who are infatuated by "what's called cutting-edge, civilization, [and] art," saying, "Human time is nothing." A rock never forgets that "the truly strong are the ones who watch in silence (Green Universe)."

As the poet "charge[s his] phone at night to remember the shame," clings to his heart that changes several times a day, without exception he sees a rock. It's hardened by persecution and hardship, but it doesn't hurt anyone when left alone. We finally find hope looking at the rock. "I stare at the pebbles piled up in the flowerpot. / Impure lips turn clear." This passage from "Only the Unchanging Things Save Me" therefore returns the life that's bent in a wrong way into its proper place. This is also related to the "way to reach virtue" in "From the Street, the Most Beautiful Street" and the "dream of water turning to stone" in "Cave Paintings." Rock is the being that holds dearly onto the helplessly flowing thing.

For this reason the poet writes, "I throw a rock, hear a cry. / I throw a rock, my whole body's / nestled underground like a baby" in the poem "History." This is the way a rock proves itself using all of its senses and memories. With its "mouth full of hurtful words (A Pebble's Prayer)," "to there and over there it penetrates, inserts (The Ruins Lab)." Each pebble that's scattered on the ground has a trajectory of its own built inside the body. They know how they came to be abandoned, for what reason they were abandoned and forgotten. Only they know. That's why "the rowdy metaphor / that's rolled and rolled / until disillusionment became nostalgia (Seashore Stone)" becomes more powerful with time. The poet's hand that writes it down is busy. Who will read this poem? Perhaps someone who got thoroughly beaten from the outside, someone who has to endure all kinds of humiliation from emotional labor or is frustrated from the inability to express their feelings.

"Those with a damaged soul read poetry. They wail, calling their friend and anxiety, boast in a loud voice. It's the day we see a shooting star, the day I return to another life (Bolt)." The night of the shooting star, those who dream of a different life will all dream of a rock, of becoming a rock. They'll speak more loudly, more clearly in silence that a rock's not just a rock when the origin is viewed in far sight, and that's when the story contained in a rock will finally be heard.

Once more on this day, rock passes through "the night [that] reminds me of you who has the word 'forgiveness'" with "a hard body that's being shaved for millions of years (The Story of Misreading)." Barely but desperately.

PRAISE FOR LEE JAE HOON

It seems that the reflective poems in *Biological Tears* (2021) combine poetic signs such as the revelationistic interpretation of reality through divine experiences, expression of self-consciousness about words, and the unique mythical imagination in Lee Jae hoon's first poetry collection *A Report on the Tribe Where My First Word Lives* (2005). In other words, the works show that the essence of sadness symbolized by tears doesn't lie in abstract pain but in transforming it into a concrete part of life, show an in-depth shift in meaning—the truth in shift in meaning that sadness doesn't impoverish us but is an unavoidable canyon that makes us proceed as a newborn being. *Biological Tears* is a weighty poetry collection that conveys the important moment of Lee's line of sight and delicate touch coming into this world.

If writing poetry is an act of planting silence between the lines and poetry the representation of philosophy that painfully estimates and contemplates that depth, then the existence of poetry itself must be a blessing. Lee's poetry is a very grateful sign that invites us to the time and space of such contemplation.

from the 13th Kim Manjung Literary Award commentary
(judges Moon Jeonghee & Lee Jaemoo)

The language in Lee's poetry isn't about dreams of running from torturous reality but of enduring the reality. The world of disillusionment stimulates and arouses his mythological, anthropological imagination. As he loses his horns, gets slashed in the sly, hypocritical, violent reality, he carves lengthy time on his body, recites the night, reads pain from before primitive senses, from a hash to a dirty flower in bloom, from grass to music.

Jeong Jaehak, praise for the poetry collection *Insect Mythology*

The knotty voice that lingers around the base of this poetry collection comprises a mixture of a daily worker's fatigue, a debauchee's guilt, an autodidact's pride, and a poet's spirit. The poet's desire for extinction is caused by his efforts to transfer a history of sadness to a record of time, the imaginative resolution to bring the finite into the infinite. Extinction is a sacred place that is acquired only after the discovery, exaggeration, and exhaustion of sadness. Therefore, if the modern man Kierkegaard is a genius of leaps, Lee is a hero of extinction.

Cho Kangsok, "Genius of Leaps Versus Hero of Extinction," a commentary on *Plutoed*

The outside of Lee's poetics is wrapped in the nomadic, revelationistic scenery established by religious imagination; the inside is supported by the somnambulist imagination of walking in the urban desert all the while painfully ruminating his youth. In that sense his first poetry collection is not only a personal log of sacred experience that creates waves in his heart but also a nomadic report on the days of youth in which he repeatedly wandered and vomited in the city.

Yoo Sung-Ho,
"The Sounds of Revelation as Told by a Priest in a Dream,"
a commentary on
A Report on the Tribe Where My First Word Lives

K-POET
Rock Is Thunder

Written by Lee Jae hoon
Translated by Susan K
Published by ASIA Publishers
Address 445, Hoedong-gil, Paju-si, Gyeonggi-do, Korea
(Seoul Office: 161-1, Seodal-ro, Dongjak-gu, Seoul, Korea)
Email bookasia@hanmail.net

ISBN 979-11-5662-317-5 (set) | 979-11-5662-652-7 (04810)
First published in Korea by ASIA Publishers 2023

This book is published with the support of the Literature Translation Institute of Korea (LTI Korea).

K-픽션 시리즈 | Korean Fiction Series

〈K-픽션〉 시리즈는 한국문학의 젊은 상상력입니다. 최근 발표된 가장 우수하고 흥미로운 작품을 엄선하여 출간하는 〈K-픽션〉은 한국문학의 생생한 현장을 국내외 독자들과 실시간으로 공유하고자 기획되었습니다. 〈바이링궐 에디션 한국 대표 소설〉 시리즈를 통해 검증된 탁월한 번역진이 참여하여 원작의 재미와 품격을 최대한 살린 〈K-픽션〉 시리즈는 매 계절마다 새로운 작품을 선보입니다.

001 버핏과의 저녁 식사-**박민규** Dinner with Buffett-**Park Min-gyu**

002 아르판-**박형서** Arpan-**Park hyoung su**

003 애드벌룬-**손보미** Hot Air Balloon-**Son Bo-mi**

004 나의 클린트 이스트우드-**오한기** My Clint Eastwood-**Oh Han-ki**

005 이베리아의 전갈-**최민우** Dishonored-**Choi Min-woo**

006 양의 미래-**황정은** Kong's Garden-**Hwang Jung-eun**

007 대니-**윤이형** Danny-**Yun I-hyeong**

008 퇴근-**천명관** Homecoming-**Cheon Myeong-kwan**

009 옥화-**금희** Ok-hwa-**Geum Hee**

010 시차-**백수린** Time Difference-**Baik Sou linne**

011 올드 맨 리버-**이장욱** Old Man River-**Lee Jang-wook**

012 권순찬과 착한 사람들-**이기호** Kwon Sun-chan and Nice People-**Lee Ki-ho**

013 알바생 자르기-**장강명** Fired-**Chang Kang-myoung**

014 어디로 가고 싶으신가요-**김애란** Where Would You Like To Go?-**Kim Ae-ran**

015 세상에서 가장 비싼 소설-**김민정** The World's Most Expensive Novel-**Kim Min-jung**

016 체스의 모든 것-**김금희** Everything About Chess-**Kim Keum-hee**

017 할로윈-**정한아** Halloween-**Chung Han-ah**

018 그 여름-**최은영** The Summer-**Choi Eunyoung**

019 어느 피씨주의자의 종생기-**구병모** The Story of P.C.-**Gu Byeong-mo**

020 모르는 영역-**권여선** An Unknown Realm-**Kwon Yeo-sun**

021 4월의 눈-**손원평** April Snow-**Sohn Won-pyung**

022 서우-**강화길** Seo-u-**Kang Hwa-gil**

023 가출-**조남주** Run Away-**Cho Nam-joo**

024 연애의 감정학-**백영옥** How to Break Up Like a Winner-**Baek Young-ok**

025 창모-**우다영** Chang-mo-**Woo Da-young**

026 검은 방-**정지아** The Black Room-**Jeong Ji-a**

027 도쿄의 마야-**장류진** Maya in Tokyo-**Jang Ryu-jin**

028 홀리데이 홈-**편혜영** Holiday Home-**Pyun Hye-young**

029 해피 투게더-**서장원** Happy Together-**Seo Jang-won**

030 골드러시-**서수진** Gold Rush-**Seo Su-jin**

031 당신이 보고 싶어하는 세상-**장강명** The World You Want to See-**Chang Kang-myoung**

032 지난밤 내 꿈에-**정한아** Last Night, In My Dream-**Chung Han-ah**

Special 휴가중인 시체-**김중혁** Corpse on Vacation-**Kim Jung-hyuk**

Special 사파에서-**방현석** Love in Sa Pa-**Bang Hyeon-seok**